Rebirth

Elle Gee

BookLeaf Publishing

India | USA | UK

Presentation by *BookLeaf Publishing*

Web: www.bookleafpub.com

E-mail: info@bookleafpub.com

ISBN: 9789360948023

First edition 2024

To every person I've ever met, no matter how long (or briefly) you stayed: thank you for teaching me something. Yours truly, Elle Gee

Remember When

Remember when spilled milk was only a wipe
away?
"Nothing to cry about," as mamas say.
Remember when a scraped knee was a death
sentence,
Those screams as though you were being eaten
alive.
Remember when the worst you could imagine
was
Sitting alone at the lunch table, or having no one
to play with at recess because
You just weren't cool enough,
And your lunch smelled funny to your peers.
It took adolescence and many years of discovery
to develop
This thick skin, these thick thighs saved [my
life]
I am not here to worry about anyone else's life.
I am here to learn, to grow, to evolve,
To rewrite my story as many times over as
necessary.
I am here to remind the child in me,
You are brave, you are strong, you are worthy.
And even on days you feel as though you are not
any of those things,
"Keep going baby, keep going!"

Rain

I like to imagine the rain as God's tears.
He's replenishing the earth,
The trees, the grass, the clovers,
They're soaking it all up.
I should be out there, too;
Playing in the puddles,
Recklessly dancing,
Allowing my inner child to come out, for once.
Does anyone do that anymore?
In adulthood, i cannot remember the last time i
was not
Consumed with anxiety, worry over whether
I was doing it all "right."
The rain is a humbling experience,
Water your seeds so you can grow.
But remember you are still just a seed,
On this mighty earth.
You don't have to do it all alone;
In fact, you are not meant to.
Let the rain be a reminder that
You are never alone, you are always loved,
And sometimes, you must do nothing more than
Just be.
Free.

Fear

My limbs are as frozen as snow on the ground,
A slippery slope, this ice that glides under my
feet;
I keep trying to avoid the fall;
Which may be worse than just succumbing to it.
This fear is paralyzing,
Feeling stuck and lost in a maze;
I'm afraid to take the next step because it all
seems so overwhelming.
Here I am once again, starting over.
And over and over and over.
I have felt this feeling before.
I have survived so many times,
This time I need to strive for more than just
surviving.
It's this wall I hit,
I can't seem to climb over it.
What if I fail again?
But how can I fail if I haven't been here before?
It is a different instance,
I am a different me,
A move evolved me, a polished me,
A present me.
I deserve to follow through with the dreams I've
kept hiding in the closet.

As the great Martin Luther King, Jr. said,
"You don't have to see the whole staircase, just
take the first step."

Love

"It was so easy in the beginning,"
She said to me.
Of course its easy.
You're not in love yet, its only the chemical
rushes of dopamine and serotonin in your brain
making it feel so so good.
A glance of the eyes,
A stroke of her hair,
Her lips grazing across yours.
The desire is easy to achieve because you're a
mystery to each other.
But love, love is familiar.
Love is this funny thing that develops over
several years of cohabitation.
How do you go back to making it easy?
Love is effort.
We used to laugh and I can argue we laughed
until the very final moments.
"How do you know it was love, then?"
She asked.
At that point I couldn't answer any more.
If it wasn't evident in my actions, in the way I
handled your heart with care, in the everyday
mundane tasks of life,
In the way I put us first.

There are not enough words to prove love.
You have to choose it, daily.
If she couldn't see that,
Or you lost sight of that,
Or you mutually decided not to choose each
other,
Maybe that's love, too.
There is love in letting go,
No matter how painful it may sound.

Rat Race

Go, go, go, go.
Don't stop, don't look back, don't pause.
Hop onto this hamster wheel and keep those gears
Turning, turning, turning.
You receive a promotion at work so that must mean
You deserve that new car,
That shiny new thing you will probably forget
about nine months from now
When your next performance evaluation is
brought up once again.
Let them rate you from 1-10 and measure you amongst
How good enough you are amongst your peers.
And then it's onto the next thing you can get
your hands on.
The more you earn, the more you "need"
The world will have you thinking these things
are important.
Consume, consume, consume!
If only we would stop spinning, stop churning,
Stop breaking our backs to earn what we think
we need,
So that we may see the truth.

You, on your own, at your core, are enough;
In your purest form of light.
You do not need six-figure salaries to fuel seven,
eight-figure incomes,
To reassure you of your worth.
Maybe it is nice, but that hustle is not
sustainable.
Remember that you will be nothing more than
Decomposed flesh to replenish the dirt in the
ground.
We always think we have more time to enjoy
these things.
Is it worth it if we are working all the time?

Hard Truth

Its more fun here, in the oblivion.
Holding onto false hopes,
Waiting for a miracle,
Blaming it all on life's circumstances.
Lacking the courage to be accountable for
Your part in your life.
You cannot control what happens to you,
But you have every right to control how you
react to it.
You hold the power in your choices, your
decisions.
There have been many who've tried to break
you,
Don't you dare let them win.
Keep going.
Why? You may ask yourself.
Because you deserve it.
Beautiful human, you deserve every good thing,
every great thing coming your way.
Let it.

Redwoods

If only the stillness of the trees could teach my limbs,
My mind, how to pause.
To remain present in every footstep,
As the wind swoops the leaves leaving the breeze longing for intention.
There is nowhere else to be, but amongst the timber giants,
Dancing, basking only in the quiet.
If you listen closely enough,
You might recognize their song, their peace.
This is the moment to revel in its glory,
For its time on earth is fleeting.
Even so, it is grateful with every ring upon its trunk,
As I learn to savor every breath;
Inhale deeply, exhale slowly;
In order to feel life's sweetest callings as my feet caress the ground.
There is no place I'd rather be, than in the here and now;
marveling in its greatness.

Maths

If only love were like calculus.
See calculus is not an easy math to master,
But at least there's always an answer.
But love, you see, can't always be
Rationalized as easily as an algebraic function.
Love is more like fiction and fairytales
And cheesy romantic comedies;
They only show you the good parts in the
movies;
No one wants to see the reality after the end
credits.
Love is a disaster waiting to happen.
It's more complicated then long division,
Because you may see it one way,
But there's a million other things to factor.
The fact is: love is work.
Day in and day out, there will be doubts.
You can't just substitute her in with a number
and solve for ex.
Because this heart beating in my chest can't
understand,
Can't come up with the best solution.
'Cause unlike mathematics, love is just an
illusion.

If

If I were to pause,
If I were to do nothing more then breathe,
If I were to contemplate a little too long,
I might feel the ground shatter from beneath my feet.
I might not be able to stop the tears.
So I run as far away from it in my mind and in my heart,
And my body is set on autopilot,
Going through the motions of life.
Grief is such a thing to be felt, at this point, so deeply felt,
It is much too real for me to come to terms with
So instead, I don't.
I will give myself the patience, grace, and mercy
To let go and let things just be.
I will not wait or ponder or think.
Breathe.

Choices

I decided I better not decide
Before I try
Confiding in you
Because we were strangers,
Then acquaintances,
Then friends,
I decided I better not hide,
Before I show
Compassion for you
Because I didn't before,
I didn't give it a second thought
Then you became this
Fantastic enigma
Alluring mystery
Exceptional beauty
I decided I better not lie,
Before I am honest with you.
Because I need to live my truth.
Because I need to face my feelings.
Despite my worries about the outcome
I decided I want you to know
Just how much I want you
And I shouldn't be ashamed of that.

Carry On

Everyday you're there
In my head like a catchy song
I keep your number in my phone because
I know it by heart, anyways
Sometimes I even miss you
I start to write that text
Hey ho..
Ho..w are you doing
But I never hit send because
I know we're better off this way
It's not like I want you back
It's not like I'm stuck in the past
Everything I wanted to say
I've said a million times before
But it'd be a lie to say
I don't love you anymore
I'll always love you to some capacity
My heart won't let me forget it
And all I can do is live with it
Endure it
And keep on living my life
The way I've been doing.

Ironic

When I was a kid,
I looked at my mom and thought she knew
everything.
Adults have all the answers, right?
Then I became the adult where I realized,
We are all still just children on the inside, but in
the vessel of adult bodies.
We don't ever stop wondering
Whether we're making the right choices for our
children,
Let alone for ourselves.
The young version of me likes to come out
And play hooky from all the adult things,
The child in me was in such a rush for -
Work, romance, fast cars, and a big house.
The ironic thing about life as an adult is the fact
that you would give the world to be a kid again.
No bills, responsibilities, or obligations.
These are the days I look a little bit closer in the
mirror,
And I remind myself it's okay
To admit I still don't know,
To realize I may never have all the answers,
To be content even comfortable living in the
uncertainty,
Or maybe; the flexibility of life.
Just go with it.

What Therapy Taught Me

How you feel is valid
How you choose to react is your responsibility
How letting go graciously is a gift
How expressing how you feel is necessary
How what you say is far less significant then
how you say it
How it's okay to talk about it,
How to make space for the discomfort that will
come in the form of
Yelling, tears, and word vomit.
It's not a bad life, just one bad day sometimes
sewn into a series of bad weeks, or months
maybe years.
The secret is to find the silver linings.

Kismet

Today I met a yogi at the library
Whom proceeded to have me sit in a meeting
room with him.
He pointed to a visual explaining enlightenment
And the left and right sides of your body and
what they represent at each level.
"Close your eyes," he said.
As he taught me cool and hot and how to
achieve
Balance.
Apparently, I am very imbalanced,
As I felt the heat radiate from the top of my head
vice a cooling effect of a breeze.
More so than the balance,
I sat there and learned to empty my mind.
Between each breath, I was instructed to say
"I release all those who have wronged me or I
have wronged. I am ready to let go and receive
blessings. I let go of any guilt and I forgive all"
There is so much heaviness he seemed to
alleviate in me in those 20 minutes.
He wouldn't let up reminding me to go home
and soak my feet in salt water nightly.
He said this would cleanse me and make me
much healthier.
I will have to try it.

Ziggy

Zigzigmajigjig-
My favorite senior puppy who is now our angel.
My fur nephew I never knew I could love so
much.
You weren't my baby,
You were my sister's baby.
Still our baby, all the same.
I think about your whole life hunting those wild
hogs in Texas.
I remember your bowed legs and your rough
hair.
How could such a sweet animal
Be used for such a rough, ruff life.
Your gentle sweet demeanor, your teethless
mouth, the wagon they'd pull you in when you
were too fatigued to complete your
neighborhood walk.
That day I saw you roll that basketball around
the yard,
Then eagerly trespass the garden bed for a fresh
tomato.
You are missed and never forgotten.

Honest

Randomly from time to time
When I'm in the checkout line at Trader Joe's,
Or Driving down the road,
Or enjoying a song,
You come to invade my thoughts.
Sometimes I burst out in tears,
Whilst other times, I find myself laughing
uncontrollably
Recollecting some of our best moments.
Like that time in LA when a car followed us into
the gated parking lot of our hotel,
Not realizing it was reserved parking nor that
they needed a gate key to exit.
I bust out laughing to that all the time,
Remembering how the girl came out of her car
waving aimlessly
While we awkwardly tried not to stare.
We stared at each other laughing so hard.
I will always appreciate that we could laugh at
everything together,
Even in the times we'd argue or be annoyed.
I miss that the most.
I miss you.

Salad

The fact of the matter is:
Our love wasn't anything special.
It was ordinary as ordinary gets.
We are regular humans,
Navigating life,
Eating this elephant,
One bite at a time.
Some days we are chomping away like Caesar
salad,
Other days, these plates get pushed to the side,
My plate is much too full
To stomach another bite.
I may have really loved this salad,
Until I ate up to my chin in romaine lettuce.
But these croutons are for crunching,
Craving, or cringing.
It's not as glamorous as the movies.
See love is as ordinary as this salad,
But I savored every drop of that dressing,
Before ever realizing the secret ingredient:
Anchovies!
I knew there was something fishy about how we
went about it.
I'm not certain whether I'll be vegan again.

Your Gift

I will close my eyes and make this a ritual
Thanking the universe for
Lifting my spirits to outer space.
I used to see nothing but darkness,
Nowadays, I focus on the stars.
The galaxies humble me as I remember,
I am just that one tiny minuscule,
Immature little star,
Compared to the ones in the sky.
I will keep my light on,
Continuing to shed my light towards what I'm
grateful for.
And if the day comes I return to dust,
I must live content with what I've contributed to
this earth, otherworldly time,
How do we measure the meaning to it all?
You are but one star with one life whose one
purpose is to shine in your purest form;
To inspire greatness and purity to all who
experience you.
That's it. Do not overthink it and make it
complicated.
Your light shines even when you do not notice
it's impact.

Do good where you can, let go where you
cannot.
Above all else,
Love yourself where you're at so as someone
may find the courage to do the same.

Insert Popular Coffee Chain Name (Here).

I don't even like their coffee,
I come here for the sugar-high.
Can I get the not-so-secret pink drink, extra
pump, please?
PLEASE!
I come here to hear the coffee shop
conversations:
Sometimes it's neighborhood gossip ,
About the divorcee that moved into unit 0729,
Condo walls talk much more loudly then you
think.
Other times, it's about their morning run,
Or the mysterious back mole,
Or their kid's classmate that pushed them on the
playground.
I don't come here for the coffee.
I come here hoping I'll find my sanity,
I come here to remind me,
Sometimes I've been lonely way too long,
Staring at the walls of my apartment.
I come here and I find comfort
In the mundanity of the human experience.

Rebirth

Some people hate routine.
I thought I was one of those people.
I thought how boring, how cruel to live such a
regular life!
The older I get, the more I can appreciate it all.
It's the simple things, really, that we should get
back to.
Hand-ground coffee beans steeped in pourover.
Sugar-in-the-raw,
Waking up and being able to water my plants.
Waking up and my back not aching nor my
lungs struggling for a breath.
A doctor once tried to tell me I have
emphysema.
I found out later I was much too young.
It's just wheezing and an albuterol inhaler for
life!
Still, what I realized was:
It's the small habits stacked over a long period
of time,
The rituals that make life so precious.
I look forward to every bit of average life I get
to have.
It's in these moments, I find peace.

www.ingramcontent.com/pod-product-compliance
Lightning Source LLC
La Vergne TN
LVHW050504210726

843509LV00015BA/2987